ANNE FRANK:
The Diary of a Young Girl

36 안네의 일기

Anne Frank

ɒted by **Carolyn S. Hyatt**
rated by **Lee Ill-Sun**

Copyright © WORLDCOM 2005

Published in Korea in 2005 by WORLDCOM

All rights reserved. No part of this publication may be reproduced, stored in a retrieval system, or transmitted in any form or by any means, electronic, mechanical, photocopying, recording, or otherwise, without the prior written permission of the publisher.

Printed and distributed by WORLDCOM

작가와 작품 설명

유태인 소녀 안네 프랑크(Anne Frank 1929~1945)는 독일 프랑크프루트에서 태어났다. 안네가 4살 되던 해 독일에 히틀러 정권이 들어서면서 유태인들을 향한 탄압이 시작되었다.

안네의 가족은 탄압을 피해 네덜란드의 암스테르담으로 이주했다. 1941년에 독일이 네덜란드를 점령하고, 히틀러는 유태인 말살 정책을 공표했다. 안네가 13세 되던 1942년 7월, 프랑크 일가와 반 단 일가는 은신처로 숨어들었다. 안네는 은신처가 게쉬타포에 의해 발각되기 사흘 전까지 2년 2개월간 일기를 썼다. 1945년 네덜란드가 해방되기 두 달 전에 베르겐벨젠 수용소에서 안네는 숨을 거두었다.

은신처의 유일한 생존자인 안네의 아버지 오토 프랑크는 전쟁의 참혹함을 알리기 위해 안네의 일기를 출간했다.

작품 설명

1942년 6월 14일, 생일 선물로 일기장을 받은 안네는 일기를 쓰기 시작한다. 안네는 일기장에게 키티라는 이름을 지어 주고, 키티는 곧 안네의 가장 소중한 친구가 된다. 무더운 여름날 독일군의 탄압을 피해 안네는 은신처에서 숨어 살기 시작한다. 그리고 자신의 외로움, 행복, 피터를 향한 감정들을 키티에게 얘기한다. 전쟁과 은신처 생활이라는, 어린 소녀가 감당하기 힘든 현실 속에서 안네는 희망과 용기를 찾으려 노력한다.

Introduction

Hello, and thank you for your interest in Worldcom's Story House! I hope you and your children enjoy the stories and characters we present to you here.

These Fairy tales have been passed down from parent to child for generations and generations. They usually teach a lesson. They teach the values that are important in every culture; like being kind, generous and helpful to others. They show that looks can be deceiving. Something beautiful, can be cruel and evil. But something ugly, can be good and loving. They also teach the value of patience. Rewards for good deeds don't always come quickly. But be patient, and the good deeds you do will bring good deeds to you. And if you keep working hard, your efforts will pay off.

I have tried my best to re-tell these stories in modern and natural English, without being too complicated or too hard. Most middle and high school children can read these stories. But I hope that parents and other adults will enjoy reading these books with their children too. There are interesting parts in each story. I hope there is enough that everyone will enjoy reading the story and listening to the native speakers.

Again, thank you for joining us in Story House. We hope you enjoy your stay.

이 책을 펴내며

안녕하세요. 월드컴의 Story House에 오신 것을 환영합니다. 부디 여러분과 여러분의 자녀들이 이 책이 들려주는 이야기들을 만끽하시길 바랍니다.

이 동화들은 부모에서 아이들에게로 여러 세대에 걸쳐 전해내려 온 이야기로서 교훈을 담고 있습니다. 이웃에게 친절하고 서로 도우면서 아낌없이 베푸는 것, 이러한 가치관의 중요성을 일깨워 주죠. 이러한 것들은 때때로 반대로 표현되기도 합니다. 겉보기에는 아름답지만 잔인하고 사악할 수 있으며, 비록 흉칙하게 보여도 착하고 사랑을 베푸는 사람일 수 있다는 것입니다. 이러한 이야기들은 우리에게 인내의 가치를 일깨워 주기도 합니다. 선한 행동의 대가는 그 즉시 되돌아오지 않습니다. 그러나 참고 기다린다면, 여러분의 선한 행동은 보답을 받을 것입니다. 그리고 열심히 노력한다면 그에 상응하는 결과를 얻을 것입니다.

저는 이 이야기들을 너무 복잡하거나 어렵지 않도록 현대적이고 자연스러운 영어로 전달하기 위해 최선을 다했습니다. 이 책은 중·고등학교 수준의 학생이라면 누구든지 읽을 수 있습니다. 그러나 부모님을 비롯한 모든 이들이 자녀분들과 함께 이 책을 즐길 수 있기를 바랍니다. 이야기마다 제각기 재미있는 부분들이 있습니다. 네이티브들이 들려주는 생생한 이야기는 현장감을 더해 주어 자신도 모르는 사이에 동화세계에 빠져들게 될 것임을 믿어 의심치 않습니다.

다시 한 번 저희 Story House에 오신 것을 감사드리며, 계속 많은 사랑 부탁드립니다.

Lori Olcott

Contents

Chapter 1 — 8
Comprehension Checkup I — 32

Chapter 2 — 36
Comprehension Checkup II — 62

Chapter 3 — 66
Comprehension Checkup III — 92

Chapter 4   96
Comprehension Checkup IV   118

Chapter 5   122
Comprehension Checkup V   134

Answers   138
Word List   144

Chapter 1

Sunday, 14 June, 1942

On Friday, June 12th, I woke up at six o'clock and no wonder; it was my birthday. But of course I was not allowed to get up at that hour, so I had to control my curiosity until a quarter to seven. Then I could bear it no longer, and went to the dining room, where I received a warm welcome from Moortje (the cat).

Soon after seven I went to Mummy and Daddy and then to the sitting room to undo my presents. The first to greet me was you, possibly the nicest of all. I got masses of things from Mummy and Daddy, and was thoroughly spoiled by my various friends. Then Lies called for me and we went to school. During recess I treated everyone to sweet biscuits, and then we had to go back to our lessons.

Now I'll just stop. Bye-bye, we're going to be great pals!

no wonder 당연하다
be allowed to …이 허용되다
control 억누르다, 지배하다
curiosity[kjùəriásəti] 호기심
no longer 더 이상 … 않다

undo (선물을, 매듭을) 풀다
thoroughly[θə́:rouli] 완전히
recess[ríːses] 쉼, 휴식
treat A to B B로 A를 대접하다

❀❀❀❀❀❀❀❀

3 But of course I was not allowed to get up at that hour, so I had to control my curiosity until a quarter to seven.
하지만 난 그렇게 일찍 일어나서는 안 되기 때문에 6시 45분까지는 호기심을 겨우 누르고 참아야 했어.

12 I got masses of things from Mummy and Daddy, and was thoroughly spoiled by my various friends.
엄마 아빠에게서 정말 많은 선물을 받았고 여러 친구들한테도 너무 많은 축하를 받았어.

Saturday, 20 June, 1942

I haven't written for a few days, because I wanted first of all to think about my diary. It's an odd idea for someone like me to keep a diary; not only because I have never done so before, but because it seems to me that neither I—nor for that matter anyone else—will be interested in the unbosomings of a thirteen-year-old schoolgirl. Still, what does that matter? I want to write, but more than that, I want to bring out all kinds of things that lie buried deep in my heart.

There is a saying that "paper is more patient than man"; it came back to me on one of my slightly melancholy days, while I sat chin in hand, feeling too bored and limp even to make up my mind whether to go out or stay at home.

odd 이상한
not only A but (also) B
　A뿐만 아니라 B도
unbosom [ʌ̀nbúzəm]
　(속마음을) 털어놓다
bring out 끄집어 내다

patient [péiʃənt] 참을성 있는
slightly 약간
melancholy [mélənkɑ̀li]
　우울한, 우울
limp 기운이 없는
make up one's mind 결심하다

3 It's an odd idea for someone like me to keep a diary; not only because I have never done so before, but because it seems to me that neither I—nor for that matter anyone else—will be interested in the unbosomings of a thirteen-year-old schoolgirl.
나 같은 애가 일기를 쓴다니 이상한 생각이 들어. 전에 일기를 써 본 적이 없을 뿐만 아니라, 나라도—그 문제에 관해서라면 아무도—열세 살짜리 여학생이 속을 털어 놓는다고 해서 관심을 가질 것 같지 않기 때문이야.

Yes, there is no doubt that paper is patient and as I don't intend to show this cardboard-covered notebook, bearing the proud name of "diary," to anyone, unless I find a real friend, boy or girl, probably nobody cares. And now I come to the root of the matter, the reason for my starting a diary: it is that I have no such real friend.

Hence, this diary. In order to enhance in my mind's eye the picture of the friend for whom I have waited so long, I don't want to set down a series of bald facts in a diary like most people do, but I want this diary itself to be my friend, and I shall call my friend Kitty. No one will grasp what I'm talking about if I begin my letters to Kitty just out of the blue, so albeit unwillingly, I will start by sketching in brief the story of my life.

no doubt 의심할 바 없이
intend …할 작정이다
cardboard 마분지, 판지
bear 지니다, 가지다
unless 만약 ~하지 않는다면
root 근원, 뿌리

hence 그러므로
enhance (안목을) 높이다
bald[bɔːld] 단조로운
out of the blue 불쑥, 갑자기
albeit[ɔːlbíːit] 비록 …이기는 하나
unwillingly 마지못해

2 and as I don't intend to show this cardboard-covered notebook, bearing the proud name of "diary," to anyone, unless I find a real friend, boy or girl, probably nobody cares.

그리고 난 남자건 여자건 진정한 친구를 발견하지 않는 한 '일기'라는 자랑스러운 이름을 가진 이 두꺼운 표지의 공책을 아무에게도 보여 주지 않을 작정이니까, 아마 아무도 상관하지 않겠지만.

14 No one will grasp what I'm talking about if I begin my letters to Kitty just out of the blue, so albeit unwillingly, I will start by sketching in brief the story of my life.

갑자기 키티에게 편지를 쓰면 내가 무슨 소리를 하는지 아무도 모를 테니까 내키지는 않지만 내 삶의 이야기를 간단히 써 나가야겠어.

My father was thirty-six when he married my mother, who was then twenty-five. My sister Margot was born in 1926 in Frankfurt-Am-Main, I followed on June 12, 1929, and, as we are Jewish, we emigrated to Holland in 1933, where my father was appointed Managing Director of Travies N.V.

The rest of our family, however, felt the full impact of Hitler's anti-Jewish laws, so life was filled with anxiety. After May 1940 good times rapidly fled: first the war, then the capitulation, followed by the arrival of the Germans, which is when the sufferings of us Jews really began. Anti-Jewish decrees followed each other in quick succession.

Jews must wear a yellow star, Jews must hand in their bicycles, Jews are banned from trains and are forbidden to drive. Jews are only allowed to do their shopping between three and five o'clock and then only in shops which bear the placard "Jewish shop."

Jewish 유태인
emigrate[émigrèit]
　이민하다, 이주하다
appoint 임명하다
managing director 이사
full impact 여파

be filled with …로 가득차다
capitulation 조건부 항복
decree[dikríː] 법령
in succession 잇달아서
forbid 금지하다

10 After May 1940 good times rapidly fled: first the war, then the capitulation, followed by the arrival of the Germans, which is when the sufferings of us Jews really began.
1940년 5월 이후로 좋은 시절은 순식간에 사라져 버렸어. 우선 전쟁이 있었고, 네덜란드의 항복, 독일군의 진격이 잇달았고, 그때부터 우리 유태인들의 수난이 실제로 시작되었어.

14 Anti-Jewish decrees followed each other in quick succession.
반 유태인 법령이 잇달아 빠른 속도로 선포되었어.

Jews must be indoors by eight o'clock and cannot even sit in their own gardens after that hour. Jews are forbidden to visit theaters, cinemas, and other places of entertainment. Jews may not take part in public sports. Swimming baths, tennis courts, hockey fields, and other sports grounds are all prohibited to them. Jews may not visit Christians. Jews must go to Jewish schools, and many more restrictions of a similar kind.

So we could not do this and were forbidden to do that. But life went on in spite of it all. Jopie used to say to me, "You're scared to do anything, because it may be forbidden." Our freedom was strictly limited. Yet things were still bearable.

So far everything is all right with the four of us and here I come to the present day.

Yours, Anne

theater 극장
entertainment 오락, 여흥
take part in …에 참가하다
prohibit 금지하다
restriction[ristríkʃən] 제한, 제약

in spite of …에도 불구하고
strictly 엄격하게
limit 제한하다
bearable 견딜 만한

11 So we could not do this and were forbidden to do that.
이처럼 우리들은 이것도 저것도 할 수 없었고, 모두 중지당했어.

12 Jopie used to say to me, "You're scared to do anything, because it may be forbidden."
요피는 나에게 "너는 이것이 금지된 일이 아닌가 해서 무엇이든 하기를 두려워하고 있어." 라고 말하고는 했어.

Wednesday, 8 July, 1942

Dear Kitty,

Years seem to have passed between Sunday and now. So much has happened, it is just as if the whole world had turned upside down. But I am still alive, Kitty, and that is the main thing, Daddy says.

Yes, I'm still alive, indeed, but don't ask where or how. You wouldn't understand a word, so I will begin by telling you what happened on Sunday afternoon.

At three o'clock someone rang the front doorbell. I was lying lazily reading a book on the veranda in the sunshine, so I didn't hear it. A bit later, Margot appeared at the kitchen door looking very excited. "The S.S. have sent a call-up notice for Daddy," she whispered. "Mummy has gone to see Mr. Van Daan already." (Van Daan is a friend who works with Daddy in the business.) It was a great shock to me, a call-up; everyone knows what that means.

turn upside down
  거꾸로 뒤집히다
indeed 아기는 그래, 실로
lazily 한가롭게
appear 나타나다

S.S. (나찌 독일의) 친위대
call-up 징집, 소집
notice 통지, 통보
whisper 속삭이다

3 Years seem to have passed between Sunday and now.
  일요일부터 오늘까지 몇 년이 지난 것 같은 느낌이야.

16 "The S.S. have sent a call-up notice for Daddy," she whispered. "Mummy has gone to see Mr. Van Daan already."
  언니가 소근거렸어. "나찌 친위대가 아빠 앞으로 소환장을 보냈어. 엄마는 벌써 반 단 아저씨를 만나러 가셨어."

I picture concentration camps and lonely cells — should we allow him to be doomed like this?

"Of course he won't go," declared Margot, while we waited together. "Mummy has gone to the Van Daans to discuss whether we should move into our hiding place tomorrow. The Van Daans are going with us, so we shall be seven in all." Silence. We couldn't talk any more, thinking about Daddy, who, little knowing what was going on, was visiting some old people in the Joodse Invalide; waiting for Mummy, the heat and suspense, all made us very overawed and silent. Into hiding—where would we go, in a town or the country, in a house or a cottage, when, how, where…?

These were questions I was not allowed to ask, but I couldn't get them out of my mind. Margot and I began to pack some of our most vital belongings into a school satchel. The first thing I put in was this diary, then hair curlers, handkerchiefs, schoolbooks, a comb, old letters;

concentration camp 강제 수용소
cell 감방
doom 운명짓다
declare 단언하다
hiding place 은신처
suspense 불안, 걱정

overawed 무서운
cottage [kátidʒ] 별장
vital [váitl]
    절대 필요한, 극히 중대한
belongings 소지품
satchel [sǽtʃəl] 학생 가방

8 We couldn't talk any more, thinking about Daddy, who, little knowing what was going on, was visiting some old people in the Joodse Invalide. 우린 아빠가 무슨 일이 일어나고 있는지도 모른 채 웃제 인발리데에 있는 노인들을 방문하고 계실 것을 생각하고는 더 이상 얘기를 할 수가 없었어.

16 These were questions I was not allowed to ask, but I couldn't get them out of my mind. 이런 질문들을 하면 안 된다고 했지만 마음 속에서 떨쳐버릴 수 없었어.

I put in the craziest things with the idea that we were going into hiding. But I'm not sorry, memories mean more to me than dresses.

At five o'clock Daddy finally arrived, and we phoned Mr. Koophuis to ask if he could come around in the evening. Van Daan went and fetched Miep. Miep has been in the business with Daddy since 1933 and has become a close friend, likewise her brand-new husband, Henk. Miep came and took some shoes, dresses, coats, underwear, and stockings away in her bag, promising to return in the evening.

Then silence fell on the house. At eleven o'clock Miep and Henk Van Santen arrived. Once again, shoes, stockings, books, and underclothes disappeared into Miep's bag and Henk's deep pockets, and at eleven-thirty they too disappeared.

I was dog-tired and although I knew that it would be my last night in my own bed, I fell asleep immediately and didn't wake up until Mummy called me at five-thirty the next morning.

fetch 데리고 오다
likewise [làikwáiz] 마찬가지로
brand-new husband 새 남편

fall on …을 습격하다
be dog-tired 파김치가 되다
immediately [imí:diətli] 곧, 즉각

🌸🌸🌸🌸🌸🌸🌸🌸🌸

2 But I'm not sorry, memories mean more to me than dresses.
하지만 난 후회하지 않아. 내겐 옷보다도 추억이 더 소중하거든.

15 Once again, shoes, stockings, books, and underclothes disappeared into Miep's bag and Henk's deep pockets, and at eleven-thirty they too disappeared.
다시 한 번 신발, 스타킹, 책, 속옷가지 등이 미프의 가방과 헹크 씨의 두툼한 주머니 속으로 사라졌고, 11시 30분에는 그들마저도 사라져 버렸어.

Luckily it was not so hot as Sunday; warm rain fell steadily all day. We put on heaps of clothes as if we were going to the North Pole, the sole reason being to take clothes with us. No Jew in our situation would have dreamed of going out with a suitcase full of clothing.

I had on two vests, three pairs of pants, a dress, on top of that a skirt, jacket, summer coat, two pairs of stockings, lace-up shoes, woolly cap, scarf, and still more; I was nearly stifled before we started, but no one inquired about that.

There was breakfast things lying on the table, stripped beds, all giving the impression that we had left helter-skelter. But we didn't care about impressions, we only wanted to get away, only escape and arrive safely, nothing else.

Continued tomorrow.

Yours, Anne

steadily 끊임없이
heap 더미, 무더기
sole 단 하나의
vest 조끼, 내의
lace-up (구두가) 끈으로 묶는

woolly 양털의
inquire[inkwáiər] 묻다, 알아보다
strip 벗기다
impression[impréʃən] 인상, 흔적
helter-skelter 허둥지둥

🧩🧩🧩🧩🧩🧩🧩🧩🧩

2 We put on heaps of clothes as if we were going to the North Pole, the sole reason being to take clothes with us.
우리는 북극에라도 가는 것처럼 옷을 잔뜩 껴입었는데 진짜 이유는 옷을 많이 가져가려는 것이었어.

4 No Jew in our situation would have dreamed of going out with a suitcase full of clothing. 우리 같은 상황에 있는 유태인이 옷이 가득 든 가방을 가지고 외출을 한다는 건 상상도 못하기 때문이야.

Thursday, 9 July, 1942

Dear Kitty,

So we walked in the pouring rain, Daddy, Mummy, and I, each with a school satchel and shopping bag filled to the brim with all kinds of things thrown together anyhow.

We got sympathetic looks from people on their way to work. You could see by their faces how sorry they were they couldn't offer us a lift; the gaudy yellow star spoke for itself.

Only when we were on the road did Mummy and Daddy begin to tell me bits and pieces about the plan.

The hiding place itself would be in the building where Daddy has his office. Daddy didn't have many people working for him: Mr. Kraler, Koophuis, Miep, and Elli Vossen, a twenty-three-year-old typist who all knew of our arrival.

fill to the brim
잔뜩 붓다
anyhow
어떻게 해서든지
sympathetic
동정어린
on one's way to
…으로 가는 길에
lift 차에 태워줌, 도움
gaudy [gɔ́ːdi]
촌스럽게 번지르르한
speak for itself
스스로 명백해지다

3 Daddy, Mummy, and I, each with a school satchel and shopping bag filled to the brim with all kinds of things thrown together anyhow. 아빠, 엄마, 나, 이렇게 셋이서 긁어 모을 수 있는 모든 물건들을 넘칠 정도로 쑤셔 넣은 책가방과 쇼핑백을 든 채 말이야.

8 You could see by their faces how sorry they were they couldn't offer us a lift; the gaudy yellow star spoke for itself. 그들의 얼굴에서 우리를 태워줄 수 없어서 안됐다는 표정을 읽을 수 있었어. 번쩍거리는 노란 별표가 우리의 신분을 그대로 말해 주었으니까.

I will describe the building: there is a large warehouse on the ground floor which is used as a store. The front door to the house is next to the warehouse door, and inside the front door is a second doorway which leads to a staircase.

A wooden staircase leads from the downstairs passage to the next floor. There is a small landing at the top. There is a door at each end of the landing, the left one leading to a storeroom at the front of the house and to the attics.

The right-hand door leads to our "Secret Annexe." No one would ever guess that there would be so many rooms hidden behind that plain gray door. There's a little step in front of the door and then you are inside.

There is a steep staircase immediately opposite the entrance. On the left a tiny passage brings you into a room which was to become the Frank family's bed-sitting-room, next door a smaller room, study and bedroom for the two young ladies of the family.

describe 설명하다
warehouse 창고
staircase 계단
landing 층계참
storeroom 저장실, 광

attic 다락
Secret Annexe 은신처
steep 가파른
opposite 반대편의
entrance[éntrəns] 입구, 현관

3 The front door to the house is next to the warehouse door, and inside the front door is a second doorway which leads to a staircase. 창고 옆으로 현관이 있고, 현관 안에 들어서면 계단으로 이어지는 2층 출입구가 있어.

17 On the left a tiny passage brings you into a room which was to become the Frank family's bed-sitting-room, next door a smaller room, study and bedroom for the two young ladies of the family. 왼쪽에 있는 좁은 통로를 따라가면 프랭크 일가의 거실 겸 침실이 있어. 그 옆의 조그만 방이 우리 두 자매의 공부방 겸 침실이야.

On the right a little room without windows containing the washbasin and a small W.C. compartment, with another door leading to Margot's and my room.

If you go up the next flight of stairs and open the door, you are simply amazed that there could be such a big light room in such an old house by the canal. There is a gas stove in this room (thanks to the fact that it was used as a laboratory) and a sink. This is now the kitchen for the Van Daan couple, besides being general living room, dining room, and scullery.

A tiny little corridor room will become Peter Van Daan's apartment. Then, just as on the lower landing, there is a large attic. So there you are, I've introduced you to our beautiful "Secret Annexe."

Yours, Anne

contain 포함하다
washbasin[wɔ́ːʃbèisn] 세면대
compartment[kəmpáːrtmənt]
 구획, 칸막이
flight of stairs
 (층계참 사이의) 일련의 계단

canal[kənǽl] 운하
laboratory[lǽbərətɔ̀ːri] 실험실
scullery[skʌ́ləri] 식기실
corridor[kɔ́ːridər] 복도
introduce 소개하다

1 On the right a little room without windows containing the washbasin and a small W.C. compartment, with another door leading to Margot's and my room.
오른쪽의 창문 없는 작은 방에는 세면대와 수세식 변기 시설이 있고, 언니와 내 방으로 통하는 또 하나의 문이 있어.

15 So there you are, I've introduced you to our beautiful "Secret Annexe." 자, 이렇게 해서 우리의 훌륭한 "은신처"에 대한 소개가 전부 끝났어.

Comprehension

Checkup I

I. True or False

1. The diary was a birthday gift from Anne.
2. Anne never planned to show or share her diary with anyone.
3. Anne was born in 1926 in Frankfurt-Am-Main.
4. It was raining when the Franks went into hiding.
5. The Franks wanted people to think they had left in a hurry.

II. Multiple Choice

1. Why did Anne think it was strange for someone like her to keep a diary?
   a. Because she hated writing
   b. Because she thought no one would be interested in the diary of a teenager
   c. Because she practiced writing a lot in school

2. **Why did the Frank family wear yellow stars on their coats?**
   a. Because they belonged to a club
   b. Because they were proud of their Jewish heritage
   c. Because the Germans decreed that all Jews must wear them

3. **Jews are only allowed to do their shopping ⋯**
   a. on Sunday
   b. between three and five o'clock
   c. between one and six o'clock

4. **All of the following things were forbidden for Jews EXCEPT:**
   a. Jews were forbidden to sit on their sofa.
   b. Jews were forbidden in places of entertainment.
   c. Jews were forbidden to drive.

5. **What DIDN'T the Franks bring with them to the Secret Annexe?**
   a. hair curlers
   b. underwear
   c. bicycles

Comprehension
Checkup I

III **Fill in the Blanks - use the words in the word bank**
(each word is used once)

anxiety	banned	going	hear	heaps
guess	lazily	hidden	forbidden	felt

1. The rest of our family _____ the full impact of Hitler's anti-Jewish laws, so life was filled with _____ .

2. Jews must wear a yellow star, Jews must hand in their bicycles, Jews are _____ from trains and are _____ to drive.

3. I was lying _____ reading a book on the veranda in the sunshine, so I didn't _____ the doorbell.

4. We put on _____ of clothes as if we were _____ to the North Pole, the sole reason being to take clothes with us.

5. No one would ever _____ that there would be so many rooms _____ behind that plain gray door.

IV **Draw a line to connect the first half of each sentence with the second half:**

A

Then I could bear it no longer,

I haven't written for a few days,

Jews must be indoors by eight o'clock

The Van Daans are going with us,

The front door to the house is next to the warehouse door,

B

and cannot even sit in their own gardens after that hour.

and inside the front door is a second doorway which leads to a staircase.

so we shall be seven in all.

because I wanted first of all to think about my diary.

and went to the dining room, where I received a warm welcome from the cat.

Chapter 2

Friday, 14 August, 1942

Dear Kitty,

I have deserted you for a whole month, but honestly, there is so little news here that I can't find amusing things to tell you every day. The Van Daans arrived on July 13. At nine-thirty in the morning (we were still having breakfast) Peter arrived, the Van Daans's son, not sixteen yet, a rather soft, shy, gawky youth; can't expect much from his company. He brought his cat (Mouschi) with him. Mr. and Mrs. Van Daan arrived half an hour later.

※※※※※※※※※※

4 There is so little news here that I can't find amusing things to tell you every day. 새로운 소식이라고는 거의 없기 때문에 매일 네게 얘기해 줄 만한 재미있는 일들을 찾을 수 없단다.

9 (I) can't expect much from his company.
그하고 친구가 되기를 기대하기는 어려울 것 같아.

desert[dizə́ːrt] 버리다
honestly 솔직히 말해서, 솔직하게
little 거의 없는
amusing 재미있는

rather 다소, 오히려
shy 수줍은
gawky[gɔ́ːki] 얼빠진, 멍청한

From the day they arrived we all had meals cozily together and after three days it was just as if we were one large family. Naturally the Van Daans were able to tell us a lot about the extra week they had spent in the inhabited world.

We were highly amused at the story and, when Mr. Van Daan gave us further details, laughed still more at the way people can let their imagination run away with them. One family had seen the pair of us pass on bicycles very early in the morning and another lady knew quite definitely that we were fetched by a military car in the middle of the night.

Yours, Anne

cozily 편안하게
naturally 당연히
extra[ékstrə] 여분의
inhabited[inhǽbitid]
  사람이 살고 있는
detail 상세한 설명

imagination[imæ̀dʒənéiʃən]
  상상력
run away with
  …을 극단으로 흐르게 하다
definitely 분명히, 명확히
military[mílitèri] 군용의, 군대의

1 From the day they arrived we all had meals cozily together and after three days it was just as if we were one large family.
그들이 도착한 날부터 우리는 함께 편안하게 식사를 했고, 3일 후에는 마치 하나의 대가족인 것처럼 느껴졌어.

8 (We) laughed still more at the way people can let their imagination run away with them. 사람들이 그들 마음대로 상상력을 동원할 것을 생각하면서 우리는 더 많이 웃었어.

Friday, 9 October, 1942

Dear Kitty,

I've only got dismal and depressing news for you today. Our many Jewish friends are being taken away by the dozen. These people are treated by the Gestapo without a shred of decency, being loaded into cattle trucks and sent to Westerbork, the big Jewish camp in Drente. Westerbork sounds terrible: only one washing cubicle for a hundred people and not nearly enough lavatories. There is no separate accommodations. Men, women, and children all sleep together.

If it is as bad as this in Holland whatever will it be like in the distant and barbarous regions they are sent to? We assume that most of them are murdered. The English radio speaks of their being gassed.

dismal[dízməl]
 비참한, 무시무시한
depressing 침울한, 울적한
Gestapo 게쉬타포(나찌 독일의
 비밀 국가 경찰)
shred 아주 조금, 소량
decency[díːsnsi] 체면, 품위

washing cubicle 세탁실
lavatory[lǽvətɔ̀ːri]
 화장실, 세면장
accommodation 시설
barbarous[báːrbərəs] 잔인한
assume[əsúːm] (증거는 없으나)
 사실이라고 생각하다

14 If it is as bad as this in Holland whatever will it be like in the distant and barbarous regions they are sent to?
네덜란드에서도 이 지경인데 그들이 추방당하는 저 먼 곳의 잔인한 지역은 과연 어떻겠니?

17 The English radio speaks of their being gassed.
영국 라디오 방송에서는 그들이 독가스로 처형되고 있다고 말하고 있어.

Perhaps that is the quickest way to die. I feel terribly upset. I couldn't tear myself away while Miep told these dreadful stories.

Prominent citizens—innocent people—are thrown into prison to await their fate. If the saboteur can't be traced, the Gestapo simply puts about five hostages against the wall. Announcements of their deaths appear in the papers frequently.

These outrages are described as "fatal accidents." Nice people, the Germans! To think that I was once one of them too! No, Hitler took away our nationality long ago. In fact, Germans and Jews are the greatest enemies in the world.

Yours, Anne

2 I couldn't tear myself away while Miep told these dreadful stories. 미프에게서 이 끔찍한 얘기를 들으면서 뿌리치고 떠날 수 없었단다.

5 If the saboteur can't be traced, the Gestapo simply puts about five hostages against the wall. 방해 활동자들을 찾아낼 수 없으면 게쉬타포는 다섯 명의 인질을 처형해 버린대.

tear oneself away
  뿌리치고 떠나다
dreadful 끔찍한
prominent[prámənənt] 저명한
innocent 무고한
saboteur[sæbətə́ːr] 방해 활동자
hostage[hástidʒ] 인질

announcement[ənáunsmənt]
  공고, 발표
frequently 자주, 종종
outrage 유린, 학대, 폭행
fatal[féitl] 불가피한
nationality 국적

Monday, 9 November, 1942

Dear Kitty,

The biggest surprise came from Mr. Van Daan when, at one o'clock, he announced that the British had landed in Tunis, Algiers, Casablanca, and Oran. "This is the beginning of the end," everyone was saying, but Churchill, the British Prime Minister, who had probably heard the same thing in England, said: "This is not to the end. It is not even the beginning of the end. But it is, perhaps, the end of the beginning." Do you see the difference?

There is certainly reason for optimism. Stalingrad, the Russian town which they've already been defending for three months, still hasn't fallen into German hands⋯.

Yours, Anne

land 상륙하다
Prime Minister 수상
optimism 낙관론

defend 방어하다
fall into one's hand
…의 수중에 들어가다

🌸🌸🌸🌸🌸🌸🌸🌸🌸

9 "This is not to the end. It is not even the beginning of the end. But it is, perhaps, the end of the beginning."
이것은 끝이 아닙니다. 끝의 시작은 더욱 아닙니다. 하지만, 아마도 시작의 끝일 것입니다."

14 Stalingrad, the Russian town which they've already been defending for three months, still hasn't fallen into German hands…. 러시아군이 삼 개월 동안이나 방어하고 있는 러시아의 도시 스탈린그라드가 아직도 독일군 수중에 떨어지지 않고 있어….

45

Thursday, 19 November, 1942

Dear Kitty,

Dussel has told us a lot about the outside world, which we have missed for so long now. He had very sad news. Countless friends and acquaintances have gone to a terrible fate. Evening after evening the green and gray army lorries trundle past. The Germans ring at every front door to inquire if there are any Jews living in the house. If there are, then the whole family has to go at once. If they don't find any, they go on to the next house.

No one has a chance of evading them unless one goes into hiding. Often they go around with lists, and only ring when they know they can get a good haul. Sometimes they let them off for cash so much per head. It seems like the slave hunts of olden times. But it's certainly no joke; it's much too tragic for that.

In the evenings when it's dark, I often see rows of good, innocent people accompanied by crying children, walking on and on, in the

countless 셀 수 없을 만큼
acquaintance[əkwéintəns]
　아는 사람
fate 운명
lorry 트럭

trundle 운반하다, 달리다
evade 피하다
haul 소득
olden times 옛날에
accompany 동행하다, 동반하다

13 No one has a chance of evading them unless one goes into hiding.
　은신처로 숨어들지 않는 한 아무도 그들의 마수에서 벗어날 수 없어.

17 It seems like the slave hunts of olden times. But it's certainly no joke; it's much too tragic for that.
　옛날 노예 사냥이 바로 그랬을 거야. 하지만 이건 절대 농담이 아니야. 농담이라기에는 너무나도 비극적이야.

charge of a couple of these chaps, bullied and knocked about until they almost drop. No one is spared—old people, babies, expectant mothers, the sick—each and all join in the march of death.

How fortunate we are here, so well cared for and undisturbed. We wouldn't have to worry about all this misery were it not that we are so anxious about all those dear to us whom we can no longer help.

I feel wicked sleeping in a warm bed, while my dearest friends have been knocked down or have fallen into a gutter somewhere out in the cold night. I get frightened when I think of close friends who have now been delivered into the hands of the cruelest brutes that walk the earth. And all because they are Jews!

Yours, Anne

---

bully 괴롭히다
knock about 마구 패다
expectant mother 임신부
undisturbed
　방해받지 않는, 평온한

misery 비참함
wicked [wíkid] 나쁜, 사악한
knock down 때려 눕히다
gutter 도랑

2 No one is spared—old people, babies, expectant mothers, the sick—each and all join in the march of death.
노인이건, 아이건, 임신부건, 병자건 그 어느 누구도 피할 수 없이 모두 다 이 죽음의 행렬에 합류하게 된대.

Saturday, 27 February, 1943

Dear Kitty,

Pim is expecting the invasion any day. Churchill has had pneumonia, but is improving slowly. The freedom-loving Gandhi of India is holding his umpteenth fast. Mrs. Van Daan claims to be fatalistic. But who is the most scared when the guns go off? No one else but Petronella.

You'd never guess what has happened to us now. The owner of these premises has sold the house without informing Kraler and Koophuis. One morning the new owner arrived with an architect to have a look at the house. Luckily, Mr. Koophuis was present and showed the gentlemen everything except the "Secret Annexe."

invasion 침공
pneumonia[njumóunjə] 폐렴
improve 나아지다
umpteenth[ʌ̀mptíːnθ]
    몇 번째인지 모를 정도의

fast 단식
fatalistic 숙명론자의
premise[prémis] 건물
inform 알리다
architect[ɑ́ːrkitèkt] 건축가

7 But who is the most scared when the guns go off? No one else but Petronella. 하지만 총소리가 날 때마다 제일 겁내는 사람은 누구겠니? 바로 페트로넬라 아줌마야.

He professed to have forgotten the key of the communicating door. The new owner didn't question any further. It will be all right as long as he doesn't come back and want to see the "Secret Annexe", because then it won't look too good for us.

Lately Mummy and I have been getting on better together, but we still never confide in each other. Margot is more catty than ever and Daddy has got something he is keeping to himself, but he remains the same darling.

New butter and margarine rationing at table! Each person has their little bit of fat put on their plate. In my opinion the Van Daans don't divide it at all fairly. However, my parents are much too afraid of a row to say anything about it. Pity, I think you should always give people like them tit for tat.

Yours, Anne

profess …인 체하다, 가장하다
communicate
  통해 있다, 이어져 있다
get on 잘 지내다, 성공하다
confide in 신뢰하다,
  비밀을 털어놓다

catty 심술궂은
keep to oneself 비밀로 하다
ration 배급하다
divide 나누다
fairly 공평하게
tit for tat 되갚음

3 It will be all right as long as he doesn't come back and want to see the "Secret Annexe",
그가 다시 와서 은신처를 보자고 하지 않는 한 괜찮을 거야.

16 Pity, I think you should always give people like them tit for tat.
유감이야, 난 그런 사람들에게는 언제나 되갚아 줘야 한다고 생각해.

Saturday, 1 May, 1943

Dear Kitty,

If I just think of how we live here, I usually come to the conclusion that it is a paradise compared with how other Jews who are not in hiding must be living. Even so, later on, when everything is normal again, I shall be amazed to think that we, who were so spick and span at home, should have sunk to such a low level. By this I mean that our manners have declined.

The Van Daans have been sleeping on the same flannelette sheet the whole winter; one can't wash it here because the soap powder we get on the ration isn't sufficient, and besides it's not good enough.

---

come to the conclusion that
　…이라고 판단하다
paradise[pǽrədàis] 천국, 낙원
compare with …와 비교해서
spick and span 말쑥한, 깔끔한

sink 가라앉다
decline 하락하다
flannelette 플란넬
soap powder 가루비누
sufficient[səfíʃənt] 충분한

3 If I just think of how we live here, I usually come to the conclusion that it is a paradise compared with how other Jews who are not in hiding must be living.

우리가 여기에서 어떻게 살고 있는가에 대해 생각해 보면, 은신처로 숨어 들지 못한 다른 유태인들의 삶에 비해 여긴 낙원이라고 여겨지게 돼.

6 Even so, later on, when everything is normal again, I shall be amazed to think that we, who were so spick and span at home, should have sunk to such a low level.

그렇다 하더라도 나중에 모든 것이 다시 정상으로 되돌아갔을 때, 집에 있을 때는 그토록 말쑥했던 우리가 이렇게 비참한 생활을 했다고 생각하면 놀랄 거야.

Daddy goes about in frayed trousers and his tie is beginning to show signs of wear too.

Mummy's corsets have split today and are too old to be repaired, while Margot goes about in a brassiere two sizes too small for her.

Mummy and Margot have managed the whole winter with three vests between them, and mine are so small that they don't even reach my tummy.

They were banging away so much last night that four times I gathered all my belongings together. Today I have packed a suitcase with the most necessary things for an escape. But Mummy quite rightly says: "Where will you escape to?" The whole of Holland is being punished for the strikes which have been going on in many parts of the country. Therefore a state of siege has been declared and everyone gets one butter coupon less. What naughty little children!

Yours, Anne

frayed 해진, 닳은
split 찢어지다
manage 그럭저럭 지내다,
  간신히 … 하다
reach 닿다, 도달하다
tummy 배

necessary 필요한
escape[iskéip]
  도망하다, 탈출하다
strike 공습
state of siege 계엄 (상태)
naughty 못된

🧩🧩🧩🧩🧩

6 Mummy and Margot have managed the whole winter with three vests between them, and mine are so small that they don't even reach my tummy. 엄마와 언니는 겨울 내내 속옷 세 벌을 번갈아 입으며 간신히 지내고 있고 내 것은 너무 작아서 배에 닿지도 않을 정도야.

15 The whole of Holland is being punished for the strikes which have been going on in many parts of the country.
네덜란드 도처에서 벌어지고 있는 공습 때문에 나라 전체가 고통받고 있어.

Monday evening, 8 November, 1943

Dear Kitty,

This evening, while Elli was still here, there was a long, loud, penetrating ring at the door. I turned white at once, got a tummyache and heart palpitations, all from fear. At night, when I'm in bed, I see myself alone in a dungeon, without Mummy and Daddy.

Sometimes I wander by the roadside or our "Secret Annexe" is on fire, or they come and take us away at night. I see everything as if it is actually taking place, and this gives me the feeling that it may all happen to me very soon! Miep often says she envies us for possessing such tranquillity here. That may be true, but she is not thinking about all our fears. I simply can't imagine that the world will ever be normal for us again.

penetrating [pénətrèitiŋ]
 날카로운, 꿰뚫는
turn white 창백해지다
tummyache 복통
palpitation 고동, 심장이 두근거림
dungeon [dʌ́ndʒən] 지하 감옥

wander 헤매다
by the roadside 길가에
take place 일어나다
possess 소유하다
tranquility [træŋkwíləti] 평온

6 At night, when I'm in bed, I see myself alone in a dungeon, without Mummy and Daddy. 밤에 잠자리에 들때 나는 엄마 아빠도 없는 지하 감옥 속에 혼자 있는 듯한 기분이 들어.

11 I see everything as if it is actually taking place, and this gives me the feeling that it may all happen to me very soon!
모든 게 실제로 일어나는 것처럼 너무나 생생해서 이 일이 우리에게 금방 닥칠 것만 같은 느낌이 들어!

I do talk about "after the war," but then it is only a castle in the air, something that will never really happen. If I think back to our old house, my girl friends, the fun at school, it is just as if another person lived it all, not me.

We all look down below, where people are fighting each other, we look above, where it is quiet and beautiful, and meanwhile we are cut off by the great dark mass, which will not let us go upwards, but which stands before us as an impenetrable wall; it tries to crush us, but cannot do so yet. I can only cry and implore: "Oh, if only the black circle could recede and open the way for us!"

Yours, Anne

3 If I think back to our old house, my girl friends, the fun at school, it is just as if another person lived it all, not me.
우리의 옛날 집과 친구들, 학교에서 재미있었던 일들을 회상해 보면 내가 아닌 다른 사람이 살았던 것처럼 느껴져.

castle in the air 공중누각
think back 회상하다
meanwhile 그 동안에, 그러다가
look down 내려다 보다
cut off 가로막다
mass 덩어리

upward 위쪽으로
impenetrable [impénətrəbl]
 뚫을 수 없는
implore 간청하다, 애원하다
recede [risí:d] 물러가다

Comprehension
Checkup II

I. True or False

1. The Van Daans and the Franks got along well.
2. Anne thought that most of the Jews taken by the Gestapo would survive.
3. Once in hiding, the Franks and the Van Daans had no access to outside news.
4. Anne and her sister must throw away their clothes when they outgrow them.
5. Anne often talked about "after the war", but she thought it was only a castle in the air.

II. Multiple Choice

1. When did the Van Daans move into the Secret Annexe?
   a. At the same time as the Franks moved in
   b. A day after the Franks moved in
   c. A few days after the Franks moved in

정답은 p.139에

2. **What happened to most of Anne's Jewish friends?**

    a. Like Anne and her family, they went into hiding.
    b. They continued living in their own houses.
    c. They were sent to Drente by the Gestapo.

3. **How were the deaths of Jews referred to in the newspaper?**

    a. As dreadful stories
    b. As fatal accidents
    c. As innocent people

4. **What did Anne liken the rounding up of Jews by the Germans to?**

    a. To lions closing in on their prey
    b. To the battles of Churchill
    c. To the slave hunts of olden times

5. **Anne comes to the conclusion that living in the Secret Annexe is like living in WHERE?**

    a. a prison
    b. a paradise
    c. hell

Comprehension
Checkup II

III **Fill in the Blanks - use the words in the word bank**
(each word is used once)

> evading   deserted   necessary   little   Russian
> packed   German   hiding   same   sufficient

1. I have _____ you for a whole month, but honestly, there is so _____ news here that I can't find amusing things to tell you every day.

2. Stalingrad, the _____ town which they've already been defending for three months, still hasn't fallen into _____ hands.

3. No one has a chance of _____ them unless one goes into _____.

4. The Van Daans have been sleeping on the _____ sheet the whole winter; one can't wash it here because our ration of soap powder we get isn't _____, and besides it's not good enough.

5. Today, I have _____ a suitcase with the most _____ things for an escape.

정답은 p.139에

IV **Draw a line to connect the first half of each sentence with the second half:**

A

If the saboteur can't be traced

Dussel has told us a lot about the outside world

How fortunate we are here,

A state of siege has been declared

I see everything as if it is actually taking place,

B

and this gives me the feeling that it may all happen to me very soon!

so well cared for and undisturbed.

and everyone gets one butter coupon less.

which we have missed for so long now.

the Gestapo simply puts about five hostages against the wall.

65

Chapter 3

Thursday, 6 January, 1944

Dear Kitty,

My longing to talk to someone became so intense that somehow or other I took it into my head to choose Peter.

Sometimes if I've been upstairs in Peter's room during the day, it always struck me as very snug, but because Peter is so retiring and would never turn anyone out who became a nuisance, I never dared stay long, because I was afraid he might think me a bore. I tried to think of an excuse to stay in his room and get him talking, without it being too noticeable, and my chance came yesterday. Peter has a mania for crossword puzzles at the moment and hardly does anything else. I helped him with them and we soon sat opposite each other at his little table, he on the chair and me on the divan.

longing 갈망
intense 강렬한, 심한
snug 아늑한
retiring [ritáiəriŋ]
   내성적인, 수줍은
turn out 내쫓다
nuisance [njúːsns] 귀찮은 존재

dare 감히 …하다
bore 따분한 사람
excuse 변명거리
noticeable 눈에 띄는
mania 열광
divan [divǽn] 긴 의자

3 My longing to talk to someone became so intense that somehow or other I took it into my head to choose Peter
누군가와 너무나도 얘기하고 싶어서 아쉬운 대로 피터를 택하면 어떨까 하는 생각이 들었어

14 Peter has a mania for crossword puzzles at the moment and hardly does anything else. 피터는 내가 들어갔을 때 크로스워드 퍼즐에 몰두한 채 꼼짝 않고 있었어.

It gave me a queer feeling each time I looked into his deep blue eyes, and he sat there with that mysterious laugh playing around his lips. I was able to read his inward thoughts.

I could see on his face that look of helplessness and uncertainty as to how to behave, and, at the same time, a trace of his sense of manhood. I noticed his shy manner and it made me feel very gentle; I couldn't refrain from meeting those dark eyes again and again, and with my whole heart I almost beseeched him: oh, tell me, what is going on inside you, oh, can't you look beyond this ridiculous chatter?

But the evening passed and nothing happened, except that I told him about blushing—naturally not what I have written, but just so that he would become more sure of himself as he grew older. When I lay in bed and thought over the whole situation, I found it far from encouraging, and the idea that I should beg for Peter's patronage was simply repellent.

queer 야릇한
mysterious
　이해할 수 없는, 신비한
inward 마음 속
helplessness 곤혹스러움
uncertainty 불안함
manhood 남성다움
refrain 억제하다

beseech [bisíːtʃ]
　간청하다, 탄원하다
ridiculous [ridíkjuləs]
　우스꽝스러운, 바보같은
patronage [péitrənidʒ]
　호의, 친절을 베품, 격려
repellent [ripélənt] 불쾌한

14 But the evening passed and nothing happened, except that I told him about blushing—naturally not what I have written, but just so that he would become more sure of himself as he grew older. 하지만 그날 저녁은 그대로 지나갔고 아무 일도 일어나지 않았어. 나는 그저 그에게 얼굴 붉히는 것에 대해 말했을 뿐이야. 그것도 물론 전에 내가 썼던 그대로가 아니라, 그가 좀 더 나이를 먹게 되면 자기 자신에 대해 조금 더 확신을 가지게 될 거라는 정도였어.

18 When I lay in bed and thought over the whole situation, I found it far from encouraging, and the idea that I should beg for Peter's patronage was simply repellent.
침대에 누워 그때의 모든 상황을 곰곰이 생각해 보니, 속이 상하고 피터의 사랑을 구걸해야 했다는 생각에 너무 불쾌했어.

One can do a lot to satisfy one's longings, which certainly sticks out in my case, for I have made up my mind to go and sit with Peter more often and to get him talking somehow or other.

Whatever you do, don't think I'm in love with Peter—not a bit of it! If the Van Daans had had a daughter instead of a son, I should have tried to make friends with her too.

Yours, Anne

---

1 One can do a lot to satisfy one's longings, which certainly sticks out in my case. 사람들은 자신의 열망을 관철시키기 위해 부단히 노력하잖아, 내 경우도 마찬가지야.

5 Whatever you do, don't think I'm in love with Peter—not a bit of it! 일러 두는데 내가 피터와 사랑에 빠졌다고는 생각하지 말아줘. 그건 절대 아니니까!

satisfy 만족시키다, 관철시키다
stick out 명료하다
somehow or other
　어떻게든지 해서
be in love with
　…와 사랑에 빠지다

a bit of 조금
instead of …대신에
make friends with
　…와 친구가 되다

Saturday, 19 February, 1944

Dear Kitty,

It is Saturday again and that really speaks for itself.

The morning was quiet. I helped a bit upstairs, but I didn't have more than a few fleeting words with "him". At half past two, when everyone had gone to their own rooms, either to sleep or to read, I went to the private office, with my blanket and everything, to sit at the desk and read or write. It was not long before it all became too much for me, my head drooped on to my arm, and I sobbed my heart out. The tears streamed down my cheeks and I felt desperately unhappy. Oh, if only "he" had come to comfort me. It was four o'clock by the time I went upstairs again. I went for some potatoes, with fresh hope in my heart of a meeting, but while I was still smartening up my hair in the bathroom he went down to see Boche in the warehouse.

fleeting 지나가는, 덧없는
private[práivit] 개인의, 사적인
blanket 담요
droop (고개를) 숙이다
sob one's heart out
   가슴이 메이도록 흐느껴 울다
stream down
   (눈물 등이) 흘러내리다
desperately[déspəritli]
   몹시, 절망적으로
comfort 위로하다
smarten up …을 말쑥하게 하다

3 It is Saturday again and that really speaks for itself.
또다시 토요일이야. 이 말이 의미하는 바 그대로야 (언제나 똑같아).

11 It was not long before it all became too much for me, my head drooped on to my arm, and I sobbed my heart out.
하지만 얼마 지나지 않아 나는 도저히 이 모든 것을 감당할 수 없어서, 고개를 떨구고 가슴이 메이도록 흐느껴 울었어.

Suddenly I felt the tears coming back and I hurried to the lavatory, quickly grabbing a pocket mirror as I passed. There I sat then, fully dressed, while the tears made dark spots on the red of my apron, and I felt very wretched.

This is what was going through my mind. Oh, I'll never reach Peter like this. Who knows, perhaps he doesn't like me at all and doesn't need anyone to confide in. Perhaps he only thinks about me in a casual sort of way. I shall have to go on alone once more, without friendship and without Peter. Oh, if I could nestle my head against his shoulder and not feel so hopelessly alone and deserted! Who knows, perhaps he doesn't care about me at all and looks at the others in just the same way. Perhaps I only imagined that it was especially for me? Oh, Peter, if only you could see or hear me. If the truth were to prove as bad as that, it would be more than I could bear.

Yours, Anne

apron 앞치마
wretched 비참한
in a casual way
　그저 그런, 건성으로
nestle against 비벼대다

hopelessly [hóuplisli]
　절망적으로, 절망하여
care about …에 관심을 가지다
prove [prú:v] 증명하다

7 Who knows, perhaps he doesn't like me at all and doesn't need anyone to confide in. 그는 날 전혀 좋아하지 않을 수도 있고, 마음을 털어놓을 사람이 필요 없을지도 몰라.

18 If the truth were to prove as bad as that, it would be more than I could bear. 이 모든 안 좋은 생각들이 사실이라면 난 아마 참기 힘들 거야.

Saturday, 4 March, 1944

Dear Kitty,

This is the first Saturday for months and months that hasn't been boring, dreary, and dull. And Peter is the cause.

This morning I went to the attic to hang up my apron, when Daddy asked whether I'd like to stay and talk some French. I agreed. First we talked French, and I explained something to Peter; then we did some English. Daddy read out loud to us from Dickens and I was in seventh heaven, because I sat on Daddy's chair very close to Peter.

I went downstairs at eleven o'clock. When I came upstairs again at half past eleven, he was already waiting for me on the stairs. We talked until a quarter to one.

dreary[drí∂ri] 따분한, 지루한
dull 단조롭고 지루한
cause 원인
hang up 걸다, 달다
agree 승낙하다, 동의하다

read out 음독하다
seventh heaven 제 7 천국
　(하느님과 천사가 사는 곳), 최고의
　행복
quarter 15분, 4분의 1

3 This is the first Saturday for months and months that hasn't been boring, dreary, and dull. 오늘은 몇 달 만에 처음으로 지루하지도, 따분하지도, 답답하지도 않은 토요일이었어.

10 Daddy read out loud to us from Dickens and I was in seventh heaven, because I sat on Daddy's chair very close to Peter.
아빠는 큰소리로 디킨스 작품을 읽어 주셨어. 피터 바로 옆의 아빠 의자에 앉아 있던 나는 마치 천국에 있는 것처럼 행복했어.

If, as I leave the room, he gets a chance after a meal, for instance, and if no one can hear, he says: "Good-by, Anne, see you soon."

I am so pleased! I wonder if he is going to fall in love with me after all? Anyway, he is a very nice fellow and no one knows what lovely talks I have with him!

From morn till night I look forward to seeing Peter.

Yours, Anne

for instance 예를 들어
wonder …이 아닐까 생각하다
after all 결국
fellow 사람, 친구

from morn till night
　아침부터 밤까지
look forward to …ing
　…을 기대하다

1 If, as I leave the room, he gets a chance after a meal, for instance, and if no one can hear, he says: "Good-by, Anne, see you soon."　식사를 마치고 내가 방을 나갈 때면 피터는 기회가 날 때마다 아무도 듣지 못하게 "잘 가, 안네. 또 만나."하고 말해주곤 한단다.

5 Anyway, he is a very nice fellow and no one knows what lovely talks I have with him!　아무튼 그는 정말로 좋은 사람이야. 내가 그와 얼마나 멋진 이야기를 주고 받는지 아무도 모를 거야!

Monday, 6 March, 1944

Dear Kitty,

I can tell by Peter's face that he thinks just as much as I do, and when Mrs. Van Daan yesterday evening said scoffingly: "The thinker!" I was irritated. Peter flushed and looked very embarrassed, and I was about to explode.

Why can't these people keep their mouths shut?

You can't imagine how horrible it is to stand by and see how lonely he is and yet not be able to do anything. I can so well imagine, just as if I were in his place, how desperate he must feel sometimes in quarrels and in love. Poor Peter, he needs love very much!

tell 알다, 분간하다
scoffingly 비웃으며, 비아냥거리며
irritated[irətèitid] 화가 난
flush 얼굴을 붉히다
embarrassed 창피한
be about to 막 …하려하다

explode[iksplóud] 폭발하다
keep one's mouth shut
　입을 다물다
yet 그러나, 아직
quarrel[kwɔ́:rəl] 말다툼

3 I can tell by Peter's face that he thinks just as much as I do
난 피터의 표정을 보고 그가 나와 같은 생각을 하고 있다는 것을 알 수 있어.

10 You can't imagine how horrible it is to stand by and see how lonely he is and yet not be able to do anything.
너는 내가 단지 피터곁에서 그가 쓸쓸해 하는 것을 보고만 있을 뿐 아무런 도움도 줄 수 없다는 것이 얼마나 괴로운 일인지 상상도 못할 거야.

When he said he didn't need any friends how harsh the words sounded to my ears. Oh, how mistaken he is! I don't believe he meant it a bit.

He clings to his solitude, to his affected indifference and his grown-up ways, but it's just an act, so as never, never to show his real feelings.

Poor Peter, how long will he be able to go on playing this role? Surely a terrible outburst must follow as the result of this superhuman effort?

Oh, Peter, if only I could help you, if only you would let me! Together we could drive away your loneliness and mine!

Yours, Anne

---

4 He clings to his solitude, to his affected indifference and his grown-up ways, but it's just an act, so as never, never to show his real feelings. 그는 고독에 빠져서 일부러 무관심하거나 어른인 체하고 있어. 하지만 그건 자신의 진짜 감정을 숨기려는 연기에 불과해.

9 Surely a terrible outburst must follow as the result of this superhuman effort. 분명 언젠가 때가 되면 이 초인적 노력이 무서운 힘으로 폭발하고 말 거야.

harsh 가혹한
mistaken 틀린, 판단이 잘못된
cling to (습관 등이) 배어들다
solitude[sάlitʃùːd] 고독
affected …인 체하는, 가식의

indifference 무관심
outburst 폭발, 분출
superhuman 초인적인
drive away 날려 버리다
loneliness 외로움, 고독

Thursday, 16 March, 1944

Dear Kitty,

Now I know why I'm so much more restless than Peter. He has his own room where he can work, dream, think, and sleep. I am shoved about from one corner to another. That is the reason too why I so frequently escape to the attic. There, and with you, I can be myself for a little while just a little while. Thank goodness the others can't tell what my inward feelings are, except that I'm growing cooler towards Mummy daily, I'm not so affectionate to Daddy and don't tell Margot a single thing. I'm completely closed up.

Above all, I must maintain my outward reserve, no one must know that war still reigns incessantly within. War between desire and common sense. The latter has won up till now; yet will the former prove to be the stronger of the two?

restless[réstlis] 불안한
be shoved 밀리다
frequently[frí:kwəntli]
  자주, 종종
thank goodness 다행히도
affectionate[əfékʃənət] 다정한

above all 무엇보다
maintain 유지하다
outward
  외면적인, 외면의
reign[réin] 세력을 휘두르다
incessantly[insésntli] 끊임없이

15 Above all, I must maintain my outward reserve, no one must know that war still reigns incessantly within.
   무엇보다 난 겉으로는 침묵을 지키면서 내 마음 속에서 끊임없는 전쟁이 일고 있다는 사실을 아무도 모르게 해야 해.

18 The latter has won up till now; yet will the former prove to be the stronger of the two?   지금까지는 후자(이성)가 이겼지만 끝에 가서는 전자(욕망)가 더 강해지게 될까?

Oh, it is so terribly difficult never to say anything to Peter, but I know that the first to begin must be he; there's so much I want to say and do, I've lived it all in my dreams, it is so hard to find that yet another day has gone by, and none of it comes true!

But, still, the brightest spot of all is that at least I can write down my thoughts and feelings, otherwise I would be absolutely stifled!

Yours, Anne

❈❈❈❈❈❈❈❈❈

1 Oh, it is so terribly difficult never to say anything to Peter, but I know that the first to begin must be he.
피터에게 아무 말도 않고 지내자니 정말로 힘들어. 하지만 피터가 먼저 입을 열어야 한다고 생각해.

4 it is so hard to find that yet another day has gone by, and none of it comes true! 하루하루 지나가기만 할 뿐 아무것도 실현되지 않는 것을 보고 있자니 정말 힘들어!

never to say anything
 아무 말 하지 않고
go by 지나가다
none of 아무것도 …않다

come true 실현되다
otherwise 그렇지 않으면
absolutely [æbsəlúːtli] 완전히

Tuesday, 28 March, 1944

Dearest Kitty,

I could write a lot more about politics, but I have heaps of other things to tell you today.

First, Mummy has more or less forbidden me to go upstairs so often, because, according to her, Mrs. Van Daan is jealous. Secondly, Peter has invited Margot to join us upstairs; I don't know whether it's just out of politeness or whether he really means it. Thirdly, I went and asked Daddy if he thought I need pay any regard to Mrs. Van Daan's jealousy, and he didn't think so. What next? Mummy is cross, perhaps jealous too. Daddy doesn't grudge us these times together, and thinks it's nice that we get on so well. Margot is fond of Peter too, but feels that two's company and three's a crowd.

Mummy thinks that Peter is in love with me; quite frankly, I only wish he were, then we'd be quits and really be able to get to know each other.

politics 정치
more or less 얼마간
jealous [dʒéləs] 질투하는
according to …에 의하면
politeness 예의, 공손함

pay regard to …을 고려하다
cross 화를 잘내는
grudge [grʌdʒ] 못마땅해 하다
be fond of …을 좋아하다

8 I don't know whether it's just out of politeness or whether he really means it. 그가 단지 예의상 한 말인지 진심으로 한 말인지 잘 모르겠어.

16 Margot is fond of Peter too, but feels that two's company and three's a crowd. 언니도 피터를 좋아하지만, 둘이면 좋은 친구가 될 수 있지만 셋이면 떼거리로 몰려다니는 꼴이 된다고 생각하고 있어.

She also says that he keeps on looking at me. Now, I suppose that's true, but still I can't help it if he looks at my dimples and we wink at each other occasionally, can I?

I'm in a very difficult position. Mummy is against me and I'm against her, Daddy closes his eyes and tries not to see the silent battle between us. Mummy is sad, because she does really love me, while I'm not in the least bit sad because I don't think she understands. And Peter—I don't want to give Peter up, he's such a darling. I admire him so; it can grow into something beautiful between us; why do the "old 'uns" have to poke their noses in all the time?

Yours, Anne

※※※※※※※※※※

2 I suppose that's true, but still I can't help it if he looks at my dimples and we wink at each other occasionally, can I?
그건 사실인 것 같아. 그러나 아직은 그가 내 보조개를 쳐다보면 가끔 서로 윙크를 주고 받는 수밖에 다른 수가 있겠어?

8 Mummy is sad, because she does really love me, while I'm not in the least bit sad because I don't think she understands.
엄마는 나를 사랑하니까 슬퍼하시지만, 나는 엄마가 이해심이 없다고 생각하기 때문에 조금도 슬프지 않아.

suppose 추측하다
dimple 보조개
occasionally[əkéiʒənəli] 때때로
position 처지, 입장, 위치
battle 싸움, 전투

not in the least 조금도 … 않다
admire 동경하다, 사모하다
old 'uns 어른들, 노인들
poke one's nose 간섭하다

Comprehension

Checkup III

I True or False

1. Peter had blue eyes.
2. Anne looked forward to seeing Peter all day long.
3. Anne had her own bedroom in the Secret Annexe.
4. Anne had a close relationship with her mother.
5. The brightest spot of Anne's life was writing in her diary.

II Multiple Choice

1. **Why did Anne talk to Peter in his room?**
   a. Because she was dying to talk to somebody
   b. Because she wanted to tell him a secret
   c. Because she was mad at her sister, Margot

2. How did Anne feel toward Peter?

    a. She wasn't interested in him at all.

    b. She thought he was a dull boy.

    c. She liked him a lot.

3. Where did Anne usually go to write in her diary?

    a. Her bedroom

    b. Peter's room

    c. The attic

4. Who invited Margot upstairs to join Anne and Peter?

    a. Anne invited Margot.

    b. Peter invited Margot.

    c. Margot invited herself.

5. What did Anne think the "old 'uns" were doing?

    a. They were poking their noses into her business.

    b. They were jealous of Anne's happiness.

    c. They were giving her good advice.

Comprehension
Checkup III

III **Fill in the Blanks - use the words in the word bank** (each word is used once)

> nuisance daughter son dimples long
> frequently occasionally attic forbidden according

1. Because Peter is so retiring and would never turn anyone out who became a _____, I never dared to stay _____, because I was afraid he might think me a bore.

2. If the Van Daans had had a _____ instead of a _____, I should have tried to make friends with her too.

3. That is the reason why I so _____ escape to the _____.

4. First, Mummy has _____ me to go upstairs so often, because, _____ to her, Mrs. Van Daan is jealous.

5. I can't help it if he looks at my _____ and we wink at each other _____, can I?

정답은 p.140에

IV. Draw a line to connect the first half of each sentence with the second half:

A

Peter has a mania for crossword puzzles at the moment

I went to the private office, with my blanket and everything

Suddenly I felt the tears coming back and I hurried to the lavatory,

If, as I leave the room, he gets a chance after a meal, for instance,

He clings to his solitude, to his affected indifference and his grown-up ways,

B

quickly grabbing a mirror as I passed.

and hardly does anything else.

to sit at the desk and read or write.

but it's just an act, so as never to show his real feelings.

and if no one can hear, he says: "Goodby, Anne, see you soon."

Chapter 4

Wednesday, 29 March, 1944

Dear Kitty,

Bolkestein, an M.P., was speaking on the Dutch News from London, and he said that they ought to make a collection of diaries and letters after the war. Of course, they all made a rush at my diary immediately. Just imagine how interesting it would be if I were to publish a romance of the "Secret Annexe."

But, seriously, it would seem quite funny ten years after the war if we Jews were to tell how we lived and what we ate and talked about here. Although I tell you a lot, still, even so, you only know very little of our lives.

You don't know anything about all these things, and I would need to keep on writing the whole day if I were to tell you everything in detail. People have to line up for vegetables and all kinds of other things; doctors are unable to visit the sick, because if they turn their backs on their cars for a moment, they are stolen;

M.P. 하원 의원
    (Member of Parliament)
make a rush 몰려들다
immediately[imí:diətli] 곧, 즉각
publish 출판하다
seriously 진지하게, 엄숙하게

in detail 자세하게
line up 줄을 서다
vegetable 채소
unable …할 수 없는
turn one's back on
    …에게 등을 돌리다

10 But, seriously, it would seem quite funny ten years after the war if we Jews were to tell how we lived and what we ate and talked about here. 그렇지만 정말로 전쟁이 끝나고 10년쯤 지나서 우리 유태인들이 어떻게 살았고, 무얼 먹었고, 무슨 이야기를 하며 여기서 지냈는지 발표하면 아주 재미있을 거야.

19 doctors are unable to visit the sick, because if they turn their backs on their cars for a moment, they are stolen; 의사는 자동차에서 잠시만 등을 돌려도 차를 도둑맞기 때문에 왕진을 갈 수도 없어.

Burglaries and thefts abound, so much so that you wonder what has taken hold of the Dutch for them suddenly to have become such thieves.

Little children of eight and eleven years break the windows of people's homes and steal whatever they can lay their hands on. No one dares to leave his house unoccupied for five minutes, because if you go, your things go too.

Morale among the population can't be good, the weekly rations are not enough to last for two days except the coffee substitute.

The children are ill or undernourished, everyone is wearing old clothes and old shoes.

There's one good thing in the midst of it all, which is that as the food gets worse and the measures against the people more severe, so sabotage against the authorities steadily increases.

Yours, Anne

burglary 강도
theft 도둑질, 절도
take hold of 제어하다
lay one's hand on 손이 닿다
unoccupied 비어있는
morale 사기, 기운
population 국민, 인구
substitute 대용품
undernourished 영양실조에 걸린
sabotage [sǽbətɑ̀ːʒ] 파괴 (방해) 행위
authority [əθɔ́ːrəti] 당국, 권위

🌸🌸🌸🌸🌸🌸🌸🌸

1 Burglaries and thefts abound, so much so that you wonder what has taken hold of the Dutch for them suddenly to have become such thieves. 도둑들이 우글거리고 있다니, 네덜란드 사람들이 어째서 졸지에 도둑으로 타락하게 되었는지 의심스러울 정도야.

6 No one dares to leave his house unoccupied for five minutes, because if you go, your things go too.
집을 비우면 도난을 당하니까 단 5분 간도 감히 집을 비울 수가 없어.

Tuesday, 4 April, 1944

Dear Kitty,

I want to get on; I can't imagine that I would have to lead the same sort of life as Mummy and Mrs. Van Daan and all the women who do their work and are then forgotten. I must have something besides a husband and children, something that I can devote myself to!

I want to go on living even after my death! And therefore I am grateful to God for giving me this gift, this possibility of developing myself and of writing, of expressing all that is in me.

forget 잊다
besides 외에
devote oneself to
　…에 전념하다
grateful 감사하는

gift 재능
possibility [pɑ̀səbíləti]
　능력, 가능성
develop [divélǝp] 발전시키다
express 표현하다

3 I can't imagine that I would have to lead the same sort of life as Mummy and Mrs. Van Daan and all the women who do their work and are then forgotten.
내가 엄마나 반 단 아주머니처럼, 집안일이나 할 뿐, 나중에 잊혀지는 대부분의 여자들과 같은 그런 인생을 살아 간다는 건 생각도 할 수 없어.

9 I want to go on living even after my death!
난 내가 죽은 후에도 후세에 이름을 남기고 싶어!

I can shake off everything if I write; my sorrows disappear, my courage is reborn. But, and that is the great question, will I ever be able to write anything great, will I ever become a journalist or a writer? I hope so, oh, I hope so very much, for I can recapture everything when I write, my thoughts, my ideals and my fantasies.

So I go on again with fresh courage; I think I shall succeed, because I want to write!

Yours, Anne

❈❈❈❈❈❈

2 But, and that is the great question, will I ever be able to write anything great, will I ever become a journalist or a writer? 하지만 내가 훌륭한 작품을 쓸 수 있을지, 기자나 작가가 될 수 있을지는 정말 의문이야.

8 So I go on again with fresh courage; I think I shall succeed, because I want to write! 그리고는 새롭게 용기를 내서 나아가고 있어. 난 글 쓰는 걸 원하니까 반드시 성공할 거야!

shake off 떨쳐 버리다
sorrow 슬픔
reborn 다시 태어난
journalist 기자

recapture 다시 찾다
ideal[aidíːəl] 이상
fantasy[fǽntəsi] 상상, 공상
succeed[səksíːd] 성공하다

Sunday morning, just before eleven o'clock, 16 April, 1944

Darlingest Kitty,

Remember yesterday's date, for it is a very important day in my life. Surely it is a great day for every girl when she receives her first kiss? Well, then, it is just as important for me too! Bram's kiss on my right cheek doesn't count any more, likewise the one from Mr. Walker on my right hand.

How did I suddenly come by this kiss? Well, I will tell you. Yesterday evening at eight o'clock I was sitting with Peter on his divan, it wasn't long before his arm went round me. "Let's move up a bit", I said, "then I don't bump my head against the cupboard." He moved up, almost into the corner, I laid my arm under his and across his back.

date 날짜
count 중요하다
come by …을 손에 넣다

move up 옮기다
bump 부딪히다
cupboard 찬장

🧩🧩🧩🧩🧩

12 Yesterday evening at eight o'clock I was sitting with Peter on his divan, it wasn't long before his arm went round me.
어제 저녁 8시에 피터와 긴 의자에 앉았는데 곧 그가 내 어깨에 팔을 둘렀어.

16 He moved up, almost into the corner, I laid my arm under his and across his back. 그가 거의 의자 끝으로 비스듬히 앉았고, 나는 팔을 그의 등뒤로 돌리게 되었어.

Now we've sat like this on other occasions, but never so close together as yesterday. He held me firmly against him, my left shoulder against his chest; already my heart began to beat faster, but we had not finished yet. He didn't rest until my head was on his shoulder and his against it.

When I sat upright again after about five minutes, he soon took my head in his hands and laid it against him once more. Oh, it was so lovely, I couldn't talk much, the joy was too great.

We got up at half past eight. Peter put on his gym shoes, so that when he toured the house he wouldn't make a noise, and I stood beside him.

How it came about so suddenly, I don't know, but before we went downstairs he kissed me, through my hair, half on my left cheek, half on my ear; I tore downstairs without looking round, and I'm simply longing for today!

Yours, Anne.

occasion 경우, 때
firmly 단단하게, 견고하게
chest 가슴
rest 쉬다, 그대로 있다

gym shoes 운동화
tour 돌아다니다, 여행하다
make a noise 소리를 내다
looking round 주위를 살펴보다

5 He didn't rest until my head was on his shoulder and his against it. 그는 내 머리가 그의 어깨 위에, 그의 머리가 내 머리와 맞붙게 된 후에야 잠자코 있었어.

16 How it came about so suddenly, I don't know, but before we went downstairs he kissed me, through my hair, half on my left cheek, half on my ear; 어떻게 그렇게 됐는지 나도 모르겠지만, 아래층으로 내려가기 전에 갑자기 그가 내 머리, 왼쪽 뺨, 그리고 내 한쪽 귀를 거쳐 내 입술에 키스했어.

Monday, 22 May, 1944

Dear Kitty,

To our great horror and regret we hear that the attitude of a great many people towards us Jews has changed. We hear that there is anti-Semitism now in circles that never thought of it before. This news has affected us all very, very deeply. The cause of this hatred of the jews is understandable, even human sometimes, but not good. The Christians blame the Jews for giving secrets away to the Germans, for betraying their helpers and for the fact that, through the Jews a great many Christians have gone the way of so many others before them, and suffered terrible punishments and a dreadful fate.

Would Christians behave differently in our place? The Germans have a means of making people talk.

regret 유감, 서운함
attitude 태도
anti-Semitism 반(反) 유태주의
affect 영향을 미치다
hatred of ···에 대한 증오심
understandable 이해할 수 있는
blame A for B
  B에 대해 A를 비난하다

give away 누설하다, 밀고하다
betray 배반하다
go the way of ···의 전철을 밟다
suffer 고통을 겪다
punishment [pʌ́niʃmənt]
  형벌, 처벌

5 We hear that there is anti-Semitism now in circles that never thought of it before. 예전에는 생각도 해보지 못했던 반유태적인 분위기가 돌고 있다는 이야기를 들었어.

16 Would Christians behave differently in our place? The Germans have a means of making people talk.
크리스찬들이 우리 입장이라면 다르게 행동했을까? 독일군들은 사람들을 자백시키는 방법을 가지고 있어.

Can a person, entirely at their mercy, whether Jew or Christian, always remain silent? Everyone knows that is practically impossible. Why, then, should people demand the impossible of the Jews?

It's being murmured in underground circles that the German Jews who emigrated to Holland and who are now in Poland may not be allowed to return here; they once had the right of asylum in Holland, but when Hitler has gone they will have to go back to Germany again.

Quite honestly, I can't understand that the Dutch should judge us like this. I hope one thing only, and that is that this hatred of the Jews will be a passing thing, that the Dutch will show what they are after all, and that they will never totter and lose their sense of right. For anti-Semitism is unjust!

entirely [entáiərli] 완전히, 전적으로
at one's mercy ~의 마음대로
practically [præktikəli]
  사실상, 실지로
demand 요구하다
the impossible 불가능한 일
murmur [mə́ːrmər]
  낮은 목소리로 말하다

underground 지하, 지하의
asylum [əsàiləm] 피난, 망명, 수용소
judge 비판하다, 판단하다
totter [tátər] 비틀거리다
sense of right 정의감
unjust 부당한, 불공평한

1 Can a person, entirely at their mercy, whether Jew or Christian, always remain silent? 유태인이든 기독교인이든 완전히 그들 손아귀에 넘어가면, 말안하고 버티는게 가능할까?

6 It's being murmured in underground circles that the German Jews who emigrated to Holland and who are now in Poland may not be allowed to return here.
지하 운동 조직 사람들 사이에서는 네덜란드로 이주했던 독일계 유태인 중에 지금 폴란드에 있는 사람은 이곳으로 돌아올 수 없다고들 수근거리고 있어.

And if this terrible threat should actually come true, then the pitiful little collection of Jews that remain will have to leave Holland. We, too, shall have to move on again with our little bundles, and leave this beautiful country, which offered us such a warm welcome and which now turns its back on us.

I love Holland. I who, having no native country, had hoped that it might become my fatherland, and I still hope it will!

Yours, Anne

---

3 We, too, shall have to move on again with our little bundles, and leave this beautiful country, which offered us such a warm welcome and which now turns its back on us.
우리도 역시 조그만 보따리를 싸들고, 한때는 우리를 따뜻하게 환영해 주었으나, 지금은 등을 돌리는 이 아름다운 나라를 떠나야 할거야.

8 I who, having no native country, had hoped that it might become my fatherland, and I still hope it will!
조국이 없는 나는 네덜란드가 나의 조국이 되어 주기를 바랬어. 나는 지금도 그렇게 되기를 희망하고 있단다!

threat 위협, 징후
pitiful 불쌍한
move on 옮기다
bundle 꾸러미

turn one's back on
　…에게 등을 돌리다
fatherland 조국

Thursday, 25, May, 1944

Dear Kitty,

There's something fresh every day. This morning our vegetable man was picked up for having two Jews in his house. It's a great blow to us, not only that those poor Jews are balancing on the edge of an abyss, but it's terrible for the man himself.

The world has turned topsy-turvy, respectable people are being sent off to concentration camps, prisons, and lonely cells, and the dregs that remain govern young and old, rich and poor.

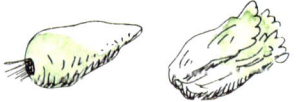

picked up for …때문에 체포되다
blow 타격
on the edge of …의 가장자리에
abyss[əbís] 지옥

topsy-turvy 뒤죽박죽으로
respectable 존경할 만한, 훌륭한
send off 쫓아 버리다
dregs 찌꺼기, 쓰레기

※※※※※※※※※

5 It's a great blow to us, not only that those poor Jews are balancing on the edge of an abyss, but it's terrible for the man himself. 우리에겐 너무나 충격적인 소식이야. 지옥의 문전에 서게 된 가엾은 유태인뿐만 아니라 그 채소 장수에게도 정말 끔찍한 일이야!

11 The dregs that remain govern young and old, rich and poor.
남아 있는 쓰레기 같은 사람들이 젊은이나 늙은이, 부자나 가난한 사람 할 것 없이 모두를 지배하고 있어.

This man is a great loss to us too. I will tell you how we shall do that; it's certainly not going to make things any pleasanter. Mummy says we shall cut out breakfast altogether, have porridge and bread for lunch, and for supper fried potatoes and possibly once or twice per week vegetables or lettuce, nothing more. We're going to be hungry, but anything is better than being discovered.

Yours, Anne

★★★★★★★★★★

1 I will tell you how we shall do that; it's certainly not going to make things any pleasanter. 우리가 어떻게 대처해야 하는지 얘기해 줄게. 확실히 상황이 더 나아지지는 않을 거야.

7 We're going to be hungry, but anything is better than being discovered. 배가 고프겠지만, 어떤 상황이든지 발각되는 것보다는 나을 거야.

loss 손실
pleasant [plézənt] 즐거운, 유쾌한
cut out 생략하다
altogether 모두

porridge [pɔ́:ridʒ] 죽
possibly 아마
lettuce 상추
discover 발견하다

Comprehension

Checkup IV

I True or False

1. Anne received her first real kiss on Sunday.
2. Anne wanted to become a writer.
3. The vegetable man was caught for hiding two Jews in his house.
4. Anne and her family ate porridge for breakfast.
5. Anne thought the worst thing in the world was to be discovered by the Germans.

II Multiple Choice

1. **Out of the following, what was actually happening in Holland?**
   a. People had their vegetables delivered to their homes because they were afraid to go out.
   b. Sick patients had to wait for their doctors to get the medicine.
   c. Cars were often stolen when left unattended to.

정답은 p.141에

2. **What was the good thing that came out of their food shortage situation?**

   a. Sabotage against the authorities steadily increased.

   b. The quality of the food decreased.

   c. Measures against the people got more severe.

3. **What did Anne say is practically impossible?**

   a. The chances of her survival

   b. Always remaining silent

   c. Her getting caught by the Gestapo

4. **What did Anne think would happen to German Jews who moved to Holland but were sent to Poland by the Germans?**

   a. After the war, they would return to Holland.

   b. After the war, they would return to Germany.

   c. After the war, they would remain in Poland.

5. **What is anti-Semitism?**

   a. Hostility toward war

   b. Hostility toward Germans

   c. Hostility toward Jews

Comprehension
Checkup IV

Fill in the Blanks - use the words in the word bank
(each word is used once)

edge	abyss	Christians	devote	children
Jews	threat	collection	abound	thieves

1. Burglaries and thefts _____, so much so that you wonder what has taken hold of the Dutch for them suddenly to have become such _____.

2. I must have something besides a husband and _____, something that I can _____ myself to.

3. The _____ blame the _____ for giving secrets away to the Germans, for betraying their helpers and for the fact that, through the Jews a great many Christians have suffered terrible punishments and a dreadful fate.

4. If this terrible _____ should come true, then the pitiful little _____ of Jews that remain will have to leave Holland.

5. It's a great blow to us, not only that those poor Jews are balancing on the _____ of an _____, but it's terrible for the man himself.

IV Draw a line to connect the first half of each sentence with the second half:

A

It would seem quite funny ten years after the war

I hope so very much, for I can recapture everything

Bram's kiss on my right cheek doesn't count any more,

To our great horror and regret we hear that the attitude

I hope one thing only, and that is that this hatred

B

likewise the one from Mr. Walker on my right hand.

of a great many people towards us Jews has changed.

when I write, my thoughts, my ideals and my fantasies.

of the Jews will be a passing thing.

if we Jews were to tell how we lived and what we ate and talked about here.

Chapter 5

Tuesday, 6 June, 1944

Dear Kitty,

"This is D-day," came the announcement over the English news and quite rightly, "this is the day." The invasion has begun!

The English gave the news at eight o'clock this morning: Calais, Boulogne, Le Havre, and Cherbourg, also the Pas de Calais(as usual), were heavily bombarded.

We discussed it over the "Annexe" breakfast at nine o'clock: Is this just a trial landing like Dieppe two years ago?

English broadcast in German, Dutch, French, and other languages at ten o'clock: "The invasion has begun!" that means the "real" invasion.

The English news at twelve o'clock in English: "This is D-day." General Eisenhower said to the French people: "Stiff fighting will come now, but after this the victory.

D-day 공격 개시일
come over 분명히 들리다
rightly 정말로
bombard [bɑmbáːrd]
  폭격 (포격)하다

discuss 토론하다
trial 시험적인, 공판
broadcast 방송
language [lǽŋgwidʒ] 언어
stiff 맹렬한, 강력한

3 "This is D-day," came the announcement over the English news and quite rightly, "this is the day." The invasion has begun! "오늘이 D데이 입니다." 라고 영국 방송에서 발표했어. 그래 바로 "오늘이 그 날이야." 상륙 작전이 시작된 거야!

19 Stiff fighting will come now, but after this the victory.
곧 격전이 벌어질 것이고, 우리는 승리할 것입니다.

The year 1944 is the year of complete victory; good luck."

Great commotion in the "Secret Annexe!" Would the long-awaited liberation that has been talked of so much, but which still seems too wonderful, too much like a fairy tale, ever come true? Could we be granted victory this year, 1944? We don't know yet, but hope is revived within us; it gives us fresh courage, and makes us strong again.

Oh, Kitty, the best part of the invasion is that I have the feeling that friends are approaching. We have been oppressed by those terrible Germans for so long, they have had their knives so at our throats, that the thoughts of friends and delivery fills us with confidence!

Yours, Anne

---

commotion 동요, 격동
long-awaited
  대망의, 기다리고 기다리던
liberation 해방
grant 주다, 수여하다
revive 다시 살아나다

approach 다가오다
oppress 억압하다
delivery 구원
confidence [kánfədəns]
  신념, 신임

4 Would the long-awaited liberation that has been talked of so much, but which still seems too wonderful, too much like a fairy tale, ever come true? 오랫동안 기다려오며 수없이 이야기해 왔던 자유가, 아직도 너무나 황홀하고 너무나 동화 속 이야기 같은 자유가 정말 실현되는 걸까?

14 they have had their knives so at our throats, that the thoughts of friends and delivery fills us with confidence!
그들이 우리 목에 칼을 대고 있는 것 같은 생활을 해왔기 때문에 동지나 구원의 손길은 우리에게 신념을 가져다 준단다!

Friday, 21 July, 1944

Dear Kitty,

Now I am getting really hopeful, now things are going well at last. Super news! An attempt has been made on Hitler's life and not even by Jewish communists or English capitalists this time, but by a proud German general, and what's more, he's a count, and still quite young. The Führer's life was saved by Divine Providence and, unfortunately, he managed to get off with just a few scratches and burns. A few officers and generals who were with him have been killed and wounded.

The chief culprit was shot.

attempt[ətémpt] 시도, 기도
communist[kámijunist]
  공산주의자
capitalist[kǽpətəlist] 자본주의자
count 백작

dvine providence 신의 섭리
get off with (가벼운 형벌로) 그치다
scratch 상처
wounded 부상을 입은
culprit 범죄자, 죄인, 범인

₄An attempt has been made on Hitler's life and not even by Jewish communists or English capitalists this time, but by a proud German general,
히틀러 암살 기도가 있었는데 이번 범인은 유태인 공산주의자도, 영국 자본주의자도 아닌 자랑스러운 독일 장군이래.

₁₀he managed to get off with just a few scratches and burns.
총통(the Führer)은 약간의 상처와 화상을 입는 것으로 그쳤대.

Perhaps the Divine Power tarried on purpose in getting him out of the way, because it would be much easier and more advantageous to the Allies if the impeccable Germans kill each other off; it'll make less work for the Russians and the English and they'll be able to begin rebuilding their own towns all the sooner.

But still, we're not that far yet, and I don't want to anticipate the glorious events too soon.

And what's more, Hitler has even been so kind as to announce to his faithful, devoted people that from now on everyone in the armed forces must obey the Gestapo, and that any soldier who knows that one of his superiors was involved in this low, cowardly attempt upon his life may shoot the same on the spot, without court-martial.

What a perfect shambles it's going to be. Little Johnnie's feet begin hurting him during a long march, he's snapped at by his boss, the officer, Johnnie grabs his rifle and cries out:

tarry 늑장부리다
on purpose 일부러
advantageous [æ̀dvəntéiʒəs]
   유리한, 이로운
impeccable [impékəbl]
   나무랄데 없는, 결점 없는
anticipate 예상하다, 기대하다

superior 상관
cowardly [káuərdli] 겁 많은
court-martial 군법 회의
shambles [ʃǽmblz]
   유혈 현장, 난장판
snap at 고함치다, 딱딱거리다

8 But still, we're not that far yet, and I don't want to anticipate the glorious events too soon. 그러나 아직은 그렇게까지는 진전되지 않았고, 그 영광이 그렇게 빨리 오리라고는 기대하고 싶지도 않아.

18 Little Johnnie's feet begin hurting him during a long march, he's snapped at by his boss, the officer, Johnnie grabs his rifle and cries out. 오랜 행군 도중에 어린 요니는 다리가 아파 걸을 수가 없고, 그의 상사인 장교가 그에게 고함을 지르는 거야. 요니는 총자루를 쥐어 잡고 소리칠 거야.

"You wanted to murder the Führer, so here's your reward."

One bang and the proud chief who dared to tick off little Johnnie has passed into eternal life (or is it eternal death?).

Do you gather a bit what I mean, or have I been skipping too much from one subject to another? I can't help it; the prospect that I may be sitting on school benches next October makes me feel far too cheerful to be logical! Oh, dearie me, hadn't I just told you that I didn't want to be too hopeful? Forgive me, they haven't given me the name "little bundle of contradictions" all for nothing!

Yours, Anne

★★★★★★★★★

8 the prospect that I may be sitting on school benches next October makes me feel far too cheerful to be logical!
10월이면 다시 학교 벤치에 앉아 있을지도 모른다는 생각에 너무나 기뻐서 차분히 말할 수가 없어.

12 they haven't given me the name "little bundle of contradictions" all for nothing!
그래서 모두들 나를 '꼬마 모순 덩어리'라고 부르는게 아니겠어!

murder 살해하다
reward 벌, 응보, 보수
tick off 꾸짖다
eternal 영원한

prospect 기대, 전망
logical 차분한, 논리적인
contradiction[kὰntrədíkʃən]
  모순

EPILOGUE

Anne's diary ends here. On August 4, 1944, the Grüne Polizei made a raid on the "Secret Annexe." All the occupants, together with Kraler and Koophuis, were arrested and sent to German and Dutch concentration camps.

The "Secret Annexe" was plundered by the Gestapo. Among a pile of old books, magazines, and newspapers which were left lying on the floor, Miep and Elli found Anne's diary. Apart from a very few passages, which are of little interest to the reader, the original text has been printed.

Of all the occupants of the "Secret Annexe," Anne's father alone returned. Kraler and Koophuis, who withstood the hardships of the Dutch camp, were able to go home to their families.

In March 1945, two months before the liberation of Holland, Anne died in the concentration camp at Bergen-Belsen.

Grüne Polizei 그뤼네 폴리차이
　（초록색 제복의 경관）
raid 급습
occupant[ákjupənt] 거주자
arrest 체포하다

plunder 약탈하다
pile 더미
withstand 견디다
hardship 고난

8 Among a pile of old books, magazines, and newspapers which were left lying on the floor, Miep and Elli found Anne's diary.
　마루바닥에 놓여 있던 옛 서적들, 잡지, 신문 더미 속에서 미프와 엘리가 안네의 일기를 발견했다.

10 Apart from a very few passages, which are of little interest to the reader, the original text has been printed.
　독자들에게 별 흥미를 끌지 못할 몇몇 구절들은 빼고 원래의 일기가 그대로 인쇄되었다.

Comprehension

Checkup V

I True or False

1. Anne heard about D-day on the evening news.
2. Anne was most excited about the invasion because she would be able to go outside again.
3. Anne's nickname was "little bundle of contradictions".
4. Anne's father was the only occupant of the Secret Annexe to survive.
5. Anne published her diary soon after the liberation of Holland.

II Multiple Choice

1. Describe the atmosphere in the Secret Annexe after they heard about D-day.

   a. Everyone was worried about what would happen to them.

   b. Everyone was sad about all the Jews who had already died.

   c. Everyone was in a great commotion when they heard the news.

정답은 p.142에

2. Who made the attempt on Hitler's life?

   a. a German soldier

   b. a Jew

   c. an English soldier

3. Why did Anne think that Divine Power spared Hitler's life?

   a. So that more Germans would kill each other, making it easier for the Allies

   b. Because all human life is valuable

   c. Because Divine Power had bigger and better plans for Hitler

4. Who was not arrested at the Secret Annexe??

   a. Anne Frank

   b. The Van Daans

   c. Miep

5. What happened to Koophuis?

   a. Koophuis died two months before the liberation of Holland.

   b. After the liberation of Holland, Koophuis was able to go home to their families.

   c. Koophuis died in a concentration camp.

Comprehension
Checkup V

III **Fill in the Blanks - use the words in the word bank**
(each word is used once)

soldier	without	Germans	died	killed
after	victory	confidence	before	with

1. General Eisenhower said to the French people: "Stiff fighting will come now, but _____ this the _____.

2. We have been oppressed by those terrible _____ for so long, they have had their knives so at our throats, that the thoughts of friends and delivery fills us with _____.

3. A few officers and generals who were _____ Hitler have been _____ and wounded.

4. Hitler has even announced to his faithful, devoted people that everyone in the armed forces must obey the Gestapo, and that any _____ who knows that one of his superiors was involved in this low, cowardly attempt upon his life may shoot the same on the spot, _____ court-martial.

5. In March 1945, two months _____ the liberation of Holland, Anne _____ in the concentration camp at Bergen-Belsen.

IV **Draw a line to connect the first half of each sentence with the second half:**

A

The English gave the news at eight o'clock this morning:

We don't know yet, but hope is revived within us;

If the Germans kill each other off;

The prospect that I may be sitting on school benches next October

Among a pile of old books, magazines, and newspapers which were left lying on the floor,

B

makes me feel far too cheerful to be logical!

it'll make less work for the Russians and the English.

Miep and Elli found Anne's diary.

it gives us fresh courage, and makes us strong again.

Calais, Boulogne, Le Havre, and Cherbourg were heavily bombarded.

Comprehension Checkup

Chapter I (32~35p)

I 1. F   2. F   3. F   4. T   5. F

II 1. b   2. c   3. b   4. a   5. c

III
1. felt, anxiety
2. banned, forbidden
3. lazily, hear
4. heaps, going
5. guess, hidden

IV

A	B
Then I could bear it no longer,	and cannot even sit in their own gardens after that hour.
I haven't written for a few days,	and inside the front door is a second doorway which leads to a staircase.
Jews must be indoors by eight o'clock	so we shall be seven in all.
The Van Daans are going with us,	because I wanted first of all to think about my diary.
The front door to the house is next to the warehouse door,	and went to the dining room, where I received a warm welcome from the cat.

Matching:
- Then I could bear it no longer, → because I wanted first of all to think about my diary.
- I haven't written for a few days, → and went to the dining room, where I received a warm welcome from the cat.
- Jews must be indoors by eight o'clock → and cannot even sit in their own gardens after that hour.
- The Van Daans are going with us, → so we shall be seven in all.
- The front door to the house is next to the warehouse door, → and inside the front door is a second doorway which leads to a staircase.

138 Anne Frank: The Diary of a Young Girl

Comprehension Checkup

Chapter II (62~65p)

I 1. T   2. F   3. F   4. F   5. T

II 1. c   2. c   3. b   4. c   5. b

III
1. deserted, little
2. Russian, German
3. evading, hiding
4. same, sufficient
5. packed, necessary

IV

A	B
If the saboteur can't be traced	and this gives me the feeling that it may all happen to me very soon!
Dussel has told us a lot about the outside world	so well cared for and undisturbed.
How fortunate we are here,	and everyone gets one butter coupon less.
A state of siege has been declared	which we have missed for so long now.
I see everything as if it is actually taking place,	the Gestapo simply puts about five hostages against the wall.

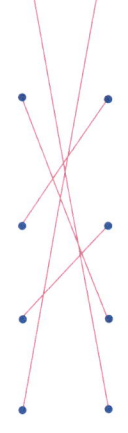

Comprehension Checkup

Checkup III (92~95p)

I 1. T   2. T   3. F   4. F   5. T

II 1. a   2. c   3. c   4. b   5. a

III 1. nuisance, long   2. daughter, son
3. frequently, attic   4. forbidden, according
5. dimples, occasionally

	A	B
IV	Peter has a mania for crossword puzzles at the moment	quickly grabbing a mirror as I passed.
	I went to the private office, with my blanket and everything	and hardly does anything else.
	Suddenly I felt the tears coming back and I hurried to the lavatory,	to sit at the desk and read or write.
	If, as I leave the room, he gets a chance after a meal, for instance,	but it's just an act, so as never to show his real feelings.
	He clings to his solitude, to his affected indifference and his grown-up ways,	and if no one can hear, he says: "Goodby, Anne, see you soon."

140 Anne Frank: The Diary of a Young Girl

Comprehension Checkup

Checkup IV (118~121p)

I 1. F   2. T   3. T   4. F   5. T

II 1. c   2. a   3. b   4. b   5. c

III
1. abound, thieves
2. children, devote
3. Chirstians, Jews
4. threat, collection
5. edge, abyss

IV

A	B
It would seem quite funny ten years after the war	likewise the one from Mr. Walker on my right hand.
I hope so very much, for I can recapture everything	of a great many people towards us Jews has changed.
Bram's kiss on my right cheek doesn't count any more,	when I write, my thoughts, my ideals and my fantasies.
To our great horror and regret we hear that the attitude	of the Jews will be a passing thing.
I hope one thing only, and that is that this hatred	if we Jews were to tell how we lived and what we ate and talked about here.

Comprehension Checkup

Checkup V (134~137p)

I 1. F   2. F   3. T   4. T   5. F

II 1. c   2. a   3. a   4. c   5. b

III 1. after, victory   2. Germans, confidence
3. with, killed   4. soldier, without
5. before, died

A	B
The English gave the news at eight o'clock this morning:	makes me feel far too cheerful to be logical!
We don't know yet, but hope is revived within us;	it'll make less work for the Russians and the English.
If the Germans kill each other off;	Miep and Elli found Anne's diary.
The prospect that I may be sitting on school benches next October	it gives us fresh courage, and makes us strong again.
Among a pile of old books, magazines, and newspapers which were left lying on the floor,	Calais, Boulogne, Le Havre, and Cherbourg were heavily bombarded.

142 Anne Frank: The Diary of a Young Girl

ANNE FRANK:
The Diary of a Young Girl
36 안네의 일기

중쇄 펴낸날	l	2009년 3월 12일
펴낸이	l	강 남 현
펴낸곳	l	월드컴출판사
등록	l	2000년 1월 17일
주소	l	서울시 구로구 구로동 222-8 (우편번호 152-848)
	l	코오롱 디지탈타워 빌란트 II 1005호
전화	l	02)3273-4300(대표)
팩스	l	02)3273-4303
이메일	l	wc4300@yahoo.co.kr
홈페이지	l	www.wcbooks.co.kr

* 본 교재는 저작권법에 의해 보호를 받는 저작물이므로
무단전재 및 무단복제를 금합니다.